MEASURE UP MATH

TEMPERATURE

Chris Woodford

 **Gareth Stevens**
Publishing

Please visit our website, www.garethstevens.com. For a free color catalog of all our high-quality books, call toll-free 1-800-542-2595 or fax 1-877-542-2596.

Library of Congress Cataloging-in-Publication Data

Woodford, Chris.
Temperature / Chris Woodford.
    p. cm. — (Measure up math)
Includes index.
ISBN 978-1-4339-7450-2 (pbk.)
ISBN 978-1-4339-7451-9 (6-pack)
ISBN 978-1-4339-7449-6 (library binding)
1. Temperature—Juvenile literature. 2. Temperature measurements—Juvenile literature. I. Title.
QC271.4.W665 2013
536'.5—dc23

2011049255

Published in 2013 by
Gareth Stevens Publishing
111 East 14th Street, Suite 349
New York, NY 10003

© 2013 Brown Bear Books Ltd

For Brown Bear Books Ltd:
Editorial Director: Lindsey Lowe
Managing Editor: Tim Harris
Children's Publisher: Anne O'Daly
Art Director: Jeni Child
Designer: Lynne Lennon
Picture Manager: Sophie Mortimer
Production Director: Alastair Gourlay

Picture Credits:
Key: r = right, tr = top right, br = bottom right, l = left, bl = bottom left,
Front Cover: Shutterstock
Interior: Getty Images: Edward Kinsman 22; **NASA:** 18bl; **NOAA:** 19; **Shutterstock:** Antoniomas 14r, Avava 8, Barry Blackburn 10–11, Patrick Bombaert 27, Christian Delbert 21tr, Discpicture 6, Adam Edwards 7, Erashov 14l, GreenStock Creative 15br, Andrey Kekyalyaynen 20–21, Jill Lang 23, Matthew Singer 12; **Thinkstock:** Ablestock 13, Comstock 24, istock 16, 26–27, LIfsize 4–5, Photos.com 17tr, Stockbyte 5tr. All other artworks and photographs Brown Bear Books. Brown Bear Books has made every attempt to contact the copyright holder. If anyone has any information could they please contact smortimer@windmillbooks.co.uk

All Artworks © Brown Bear Books Ltd

Publisher's note to educators and parents: Our editors have carefully reviewed the websites that appear on p. 31 to ensure that they are suitable for students. Many websites change frequently, however, and we cannot guarantee that a site's future contents will continue to meet our high standards of quality and educational value. Be advised that students should be closely supervised whenever they access the Internet.

Manufactured in the United States of America
1 2 3 4 5 6 7 8 9   12 11 10

CPSIA compliance information: Batch #BRS12GS: For further information contact Gareth Stevens, **New York, New York** at 1-800-542-2595.

CONTENTS

WHAT IS TEMPERATURE?

▶▶▶ **A** summer's day can feel really hot. A winter's day feels much cooler. We can tell the difference between the two using temperature.

Temperature is a measurement of how hot or cold something is. On a hot day, the temperature is high. On a cold day, the temperature is lower.

▼ This snow has stayed frozen because it is very cold. It has a low temperature.

TEMPERATURE AND HEAT

Heat and temperature are not the same. Heat is a kind of energy that things can have. When a metal bar is heated in a fire, it gains a lot of heat energy. Heat energy makes the bar hot. The bar has a high temperature because it is hot.

▶ The candle flames in these Halloween pumpkins are very hot.

Using thermometers

One way to measure temperature is using a thermometer. A thermometer is like a ruler that measures how hot or cold something is. It has a scale on its side that tells us the temperature. There are many different kinds of thermometers.

Measuring temperature can be very useful. It tells us how hot a stove needs to be to cook our dinner. It helps us know if we are sick or healthy. And measuring temperature lets us know if we need to pack warm clothes when we go on vacation.

WORD BANK   *Thermometer: a device that measures temperature*

HEAT AND COLD

▶▶▶ **L**ength is easy to measure. We can put a ruler next to a pencil and measure how long it is. But we cannot see temperature. So how can we measure it? When things get hotter or colder, they change size. If we heat a metal bar in a fire, the bar gets a tiny bit longer. If we cool the bar, it gets shorter. If we could measure how long the bar was when it was hot and cold, then the length of the bar could tell us something about its temperature.

▶ WATER, ICE, AND STEAM

Water can help us measure temperature. When it is very cold, water is frozen as solid ice. At everyday temperatures, water is a liquid. When water is very hot, it becomes a gas called steam. The water in the kettle is boiling, and steam is escaping from its spout (right).

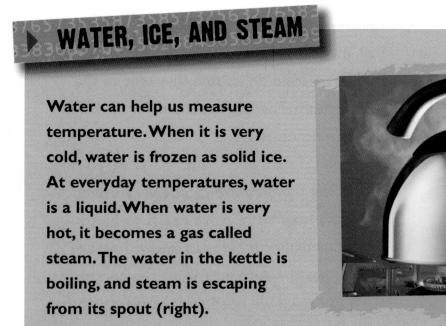

Heat changes things

We cannot see temperature, but we can see how heat changes things. We can see how heat makes a metal bar grow longer or how it makes an ice cube melt. We can also see how heat dries the earth and makes it crack. We can see and measure these changes. That is how we can measure temperature, even though we cannot see it.

▲ These icicles formed when drops of water froze to become ice.

FACT

In 2010, an icicle 27 feet (8 meters) long was seen under a bridge in Scotland.

WORD BANK *Steam: the gas formed when water is heated to 212°F*

WORKING OUT TEMPERATURES

▼ Since mercury is a poison, physicians now use digital thermometers—rather than mercury thermometers—to measure the body temperature of their patients.

We can measure temperature with a thermometer. One common type of thermometer is a hollow tube made of glass. Inside is a liquid, either mercury or alcohol. The mercury looks like a thin silver line inside the glass, and the alcohol looks like a thin red line.

A thermometer usually looks a little like a ruler. It has a scale marked on the outside of the glass. Instead of measuring length, this scale measures how hot or cold something is.

How thermometers work

The column of mercury or alcohol in a thermometer is just like a metal bar. When the liquid heats up, the column gets a little bit longer. And when it cools down, the column gets a little bit shorter.

+ – = x + – = + – = x + – =

MERCURY AND ALCOHOL THERMOMETERS

Mercury is a very special metal. At everyday temperatures, it is a liquid. Liquid mercury rises up and down inside a thermometer. Even a small temperature change makes the mercury move. An alcohol thermometer (right) works in the same way. It is not as accurate, but it is safer.

Answers on page 31.

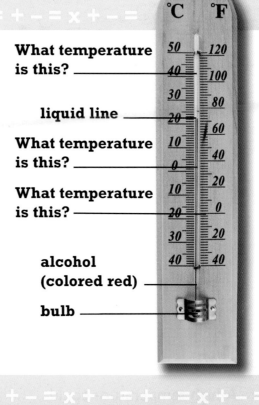

What temperature is this? _____

liquid line _____

What temperature is this? _____

What temperature is this? _____

alcohol (colored red) _____

bulb _____

°C   °F

+ – = x + – = x + – = x + – = + – = x + – = + – = x + – =

Moving up and down

So the mercury or alcohol moves up and down inside the glass tube as the temperature changes. The liquid moves along the scale, just like a finger moving along a ruler. We can find out the temperature by seeing where the liquid line is on the scale.

When the liquid moves down the scale, we know the temperature around us is lower than when it moves higher up the scale.

FACT

The mercury-in-glass thermometer was invented by Daniel Fahrenheit.

WORD BANK   *Mercury: a metal that is liquid at normal room temperature*

SCALES ON THERMOMETERS

Rulers have a scale on them marked in inches or centimeters. Thermometers also have scales on them. Instead of inches, thermometers are marked in units called degrees. A degree is one unit of temperature. A high temperature could be hundreds or thousands of degrees. A low temperature might be just a few degrees.

Fahrenheit

Thermometers can have different scales. The most common scale in the United States is

▶ **The big numbers around the outside of the circular scale show temperature in Fahrenheit.**

▼ Some important temperatures. The coldest are at the bottom, and the hottest are at the top.

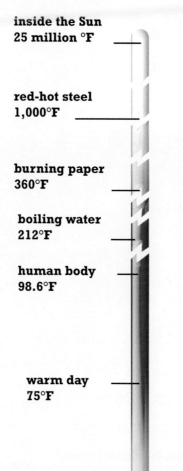

inside the Sun
25 million °F

red-hot steel
1,000°F

burning paper
360°F

boiling water
212°F

human body
98.6°F

warm day
75°F

water freezes 32°F

Antarctica −128°F
(128 degrees below zero)

called Fahrenheit. On the Fahrenheit scale, boiling water has a temperature of 212 degrees. That can be written 212°. We call this 212 degrees Fahrenheit, or 212°F. The "F" shows that we are using the Fahrenheit scale.

Freezing water

Freezing water, or ice, has a much lower temperature than boiling water. The temperature that water turns to ice is 32 degrees Fahrenheit, or 32°F. Temperatures lower than zero are extremely cold. The coldest temperatures on Earth are in Antarctica, a huge continent around the South Pole.

FACT

The coldest-ever temperature on Earth was at Vostok, Antarctica, in 1983.

Scale: a set of equally spaced marks to help us measure

THE CELSIUS SCALE

Rulers can be marked in feet and inches. They can also be marked in metric units, such as meters and centimeters. There is also a metric scale of temperature. It is called the Celsius, or centigrade, scale. It is much simpler and easier to use than the Fahrenheit scale. On the Celsius scale, freezing water has a temperature of 0 degrees. Just like a Fahrenheit temperature, this temperature can be written as 0°. We say water freezes at zero degrees Celsius, or 0°C. The "C" is a quick way of writing "Celsius" or "centigrade." 0°C is the same temperature as 32°F.

▲ Part of this waterfall is frozen ice, and part is flowing water. The water will freeze when its temperature falls to 0°C, or 32°F.

CHANGING TEMPERATURES

If you know a temperature in Fahrenheit, you can also figure out what it would be in Celsius. First, subtract 32 from the Fahrenheit temperature.

212°F − 32 = 180

Then multiply the result by 5.

180 x 5 = 900

Next, divide that result by 9.

900 ÷ 9 = 100°C

So 212°F is the same as 100°C.

What is 50°F on the Celsius scale?

To change Celsius into Fahrenheit, first multiply the Celsius temperature by 9.

100°C x 9 = 900

Then divide the result by 5.

900 ÷ 5 = 180

Finally, add 32.

180 + 32 = 212°F

So 100°C is the same as 212°F.

What is 30°C on the Fahrenheit scale?

Answers on page 31.

+ − = x + − = x + − = x + − = x + − = x + − = x + − = x + =

▶ **Steam rising from a geyser in Yellowstone National Park.**

Boiling water has a temperature of 100 degrees on the Celsius scale. That can also be written as 100°. We say water boils at one hundred degrees Celsius, or 100°C. "Centigrade" is just another way of saying "Celsius." So 100 degrees centigrade is the same as 100 degrees Celsius.

WORD BANK   *Geyser: natural fountain of steam and very hot water*

DIFFERENT KINDS OF THERMOMETERS

▶ **These two old thermometers show both the Fahrenheit and Celsius scales.**

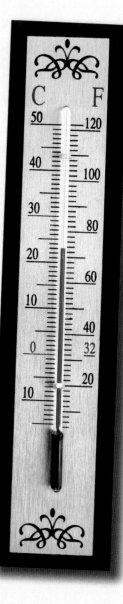

O rdinary thermometers are sometimes called mercury thermometers. There are several different kinds of thermometers. Medical thermometers are used to measure people's body temperatures. Modern medical thermometers have a digital display. That means the temperature appears as a number on a screen. Large digital thermometers on the walls of buildings show the temperature of the air outside.

Maximum and minimum thermometers

Maximum and minimum thermometers are used to study the weather. These thermometers have two tubes of mercury side by side. On any day, one side measures the highest temperature reached, and the other the lowest temperature.

▶ TRY THIS

+ − = x + − = x + − = x + − = x + − = + −

THERMOSTATS: ON OR OFF?

A thermostat can control the temperature of a room or house. It measures the temperature in a room all the time. A digital display shows the temperature. If the thermostat gets too hot, it switches off the heater. If the temperature falls too low, the thermostat switches the heater on again.

If the thermostat is set at 65°F and the room temperature is 60°F, will the thermostat switch the heater on or off? What about if the room temperature is 70°F?

Answers on page 31.

+ − = x + − = x + − = x + − = x + − = + − = x + − = x + − x

WORD BANK   *Celsius: the metric scale for measuring temperature*

15

THE GREAT INVENTORS

▶▶▶ **T**he first thermometer was made in 1592 by a brilliant Italian scientist named Galileo Galilei (1564–1642). His thermometer was an upside-down glass jar filled with air and water. Scientists soon found other substances worked much better.

Using mercury instead

A German scientist named Daniel Fahrenheit (1686–1736) also made a thermometer. In 1714, he discovered that it worked best of all using mercury. That is how the modern mercury thermometer was invented.

▶ This thermometer is based on Galileo's original thermoscope. It has multicolored glass bubbles floating in a column of water. The lowest bubble tells us what the temperature is.

Galileo's early thermometer was called a thermoscope. He took a rounded jar with a very long glass neck and warmed it up. Then he turned the jar upside down and dipped its neck into a bowl of water. As the air in the jar cooled, it shrank a little. That pulled some of the water up the glass neck. So Galileo had made a simple thermometer a bit like the mercury ones we still use.

▲ Galileo Galilei was a brilliant Italian scientist.

Ten years later, Fahrenheit worked out the temperature scale that is now named for him. Then, in 1742, Swedish scientist Anders Celsius (1701–1744) invented the other popular temperature scale, called the Celsius or centigrade scale. The "centi" part of the word "centigrade" means 100. There are 100 degrees between the freezing point of water, which is 0°C, and the boiling point of water, 100°C.

FACT

Daniel Fahrenheit discovered that the boiling point of mercury is 674°F.

WORD BANK   *Centigrade: another word for the Celsius scale*

ABSOLUTE ZERO

Everything is made of tiny invisible particles. These are called atoms. Groups of atoms are called molecules. When something is hot, its molecules move around. The hotter a thing is, the faster its molecules move. The colder something is, the slower they move.

What if we could cool something so much that its molecules stopped moving altogether? We would reach the lowest possible temperature. That temperature

HOW HOT CAN IT GET?

Absolute zero is the lowest temperature anything could ever reach. But no one really knows what the hottest is. Inside the Sun (right), the temperature is about 25 million °F, or 14 million K. On Earth, scientists have made explosions with temperatures as high as 180 million °F!

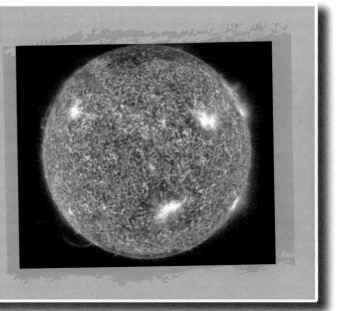

is called absolute zero. Absolute zero is − 460°F, or − 273°C. There is no temperature colder than that.

Kelvin and Rankine

Scientists use two temperature scales that start off at absolute zero. They are called the Kelvin scale and the Rankine scale. The Kelvin scale measures upward from absolute zero in degrees Celsius. The Rankine scale measures upward from absolute zero in degrees Fahrenheit. On the Kelvin scale, our body temperature is 310 Kelvin (K), water boils at 373 K, and paper burns at 460 K.

▲ Although this huge iceberg is icy cold, it is nowhere near as cold as absolute zero.

WORD BANK   *Atom: a tiny particle; all matter is made up of atoms*

WHITE HOT

When fires burn, they are often yellow or red. Lots of things change color when they heat up. If we heat an iron bar in a fire or in a very hot oven called a furnace, the iron bar slowly changes color. First it does not change color at all, even though it is getting hotter.

Color changes

Then the iron bar becomes a dull red-brown. When a metal bar is so hot that it turns red, we say it is red hot. Its temperature is then about 1,750°F. As it gets hotter still, it glows orange, yellow, and finally white. A yellow-hot bar is about 2,000°F, and a white-hot bar is hotter still.

▶ **Molten metal in a furnace glows orange and yellow. A furnace is a very hot oven that heats iron.**

▶ HEAT AND LIGHT

Hot things give out heat. We can feel the heat from a fire, for example. Some hot things also give out light. Most lightbulbs work by heating a thin piece of wire (a filament) inside them. The wire gets very hot and gives out heat and light energy. When hot things give out light, we know they are very hot indeed.

▶ The bright filament in this lightbulb is giving out heat and light energy.

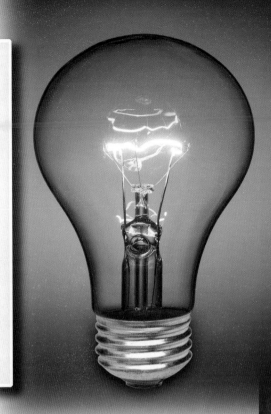

Color changes can help us measure temperature. Blacksmiths know they can shape metal only when it is very hot. They heat it until it glows orange-red. Then they know it is hot enough to hammer into shape.

In a steel foundry, white-hot molten steel is poured from a furnace into molds. The molds are the shapes that people want the steel to be when it cools and becomes solid again.

FACT

The first furnaces for melting iron were built by the Chinese 2,500 years ago.

WORD BANK   *Filament: a thin wire that produces light when heated*

MAKING USE OF TEMPERATURE

People measure temperature for many reasons. Measuring temperature is very helpful in factories. Many things, such as plastics, are best made at certain temperatures. Fresh food is also best stored at low temperatures. That helps stop the food from going bad.

▲ Animals that are active at night—such as this elephant—can be seen by using thermal cameras.

We can save energy by making houses that hold in heat. To do this, we take photographs of houses using thermal cameras. Thermal cameras see heat instead of light. They show the parts of a house where most heat escapes, such as the windows and the roof. We can then cover those areas with special materials to keep our homes warmer.

Body heat

Temperature also lets us see in the dark. Thermal pictures, or images, help rescue teams find people who get lost at night. A person's body gives off heat. So we can see a person's body with a thermal camera even when it is dark.

▶ ANIMALS AND TEMPERATURE

A cricket is a kind of thermometer. Crickets chirp more often when the weather is hotter. Listen for a cricket and count how many times it chirps in 15 seconds. Add 40 to that number. The answer you get is the temperature in degrees Fahrenheit!

◀ Lizards wake up only when the air temperature becomes warm.

WORD BANK   *Thermal image: an image that shows areas of heat*

WEATHER AND TEMPERATURE

▶▶▶ **O**ne important reason for measuring temperature is so we can forecast the weather. Earth's weather is caused mostly by the Sun. The Sun sends heat energy to Earth. That makes Earth warm up.

During the year, different parts of our planet have more hours of daylight than others. Also, when the Sun is higher in the sky, its

▶ THE COLDEST PLACES

Antarctica, which covers the South Pole, is the coldest place on Earth in winter, but hardly anyone lives there. The coldest places where anyone lives are in a part of Russia called Siberia. In the winter of 1933, the village of Oymyakon in Siberia recorded a temperature of –90°F, or –68°C.

+ – = x + – = x + – = x + – = + – = x +

MONTHLY TEMPERATURE CHART

We can see what kind of climate a place has by looking at a chart of its temperature. The high bars show the warmer months. The low bars show the cooler ones.

What temperature is it:
In April?
In August?
In December?

Answers on page 31.

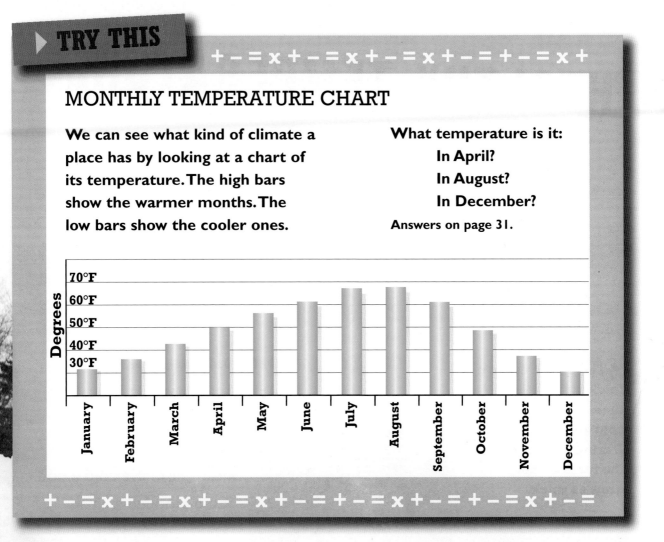

+ – = x + – = x + – = x + – = + – = x + – = + – = x + – =

◀ **Cold winter weather, with snow on the ground, is great for fun activities like toboggan rides.**

rays are stronger and warmer. So different parts of our planet warm up by different amounts. That means different parts of Earth have different temperatures. And that is what causes the weather.

Different places have different types of weather through the year. Some places are hot. Others are cold and wet. The type of weather a place has is called its climate.

WORD BANK *Climate: the normal weather of a place or country*

HEALTHY TEMPERATURES

Living things can survive only if the temperature is just right for them. Lizards, fish, and many other creatures die if it gets too hot or too cold. If a factory drains hot water into a river, the river warms up. If the river becomes too hot, all the fish in it die.

▼ These wolves have thick fur to keep them warm in the cold winter months. During summer, the fur does not grow so thick.

Cold-blooded animals

Fish, snakes, and lizards are cold-blooded creatures, or ectotherms. That does not mean they have cold blood. Cold-blooded animals

WHAT TEMPERATURE ARE YOU?

Doctors take people's temperature to tell if they are sick or healthy. A person's body temperature is normally 98.6°F, or 37°C. If people are sick, their body temperature can climb much higher. If it gets too high, they will die. Ask your mom or dad to measure your temperature with a medical thermometer (right). See how close you are to the normal body temperature.

FACT

Willie Jones holds the record for the highest body temperature: 116°F, or 47°C.

cannot make their own body heat. To warm up, they have to take heat from around them. So, lizards bask on rocks until they are warm enough to get active. To cool down, they move somewhere less hot.

Warm-blooded animals

Birds, people, and furry animals like cats, dogs, and horses are warm-blooded. Warm-blooded creatures (also called endotherms) make their own body heat. The food they eat makes heat energy that warms them from the inside. Feathers or thick fur keep warm-blooded animals warm in winter.

ESTIMATING TEMPERATURE

YOU WILL NEED

- **Several liquid-crystal thermometer strips**
- **Some things around your home to test**
- **A pencil and paper**

WHAT TO DO

Can you guess which item is the hottest?

1. Think of five or ten things around your home that you can test the temperature of. You might test:

- A sunny window ledge
- Your arm
- A cold faucet
- Different materials, such as paper, metal, or a wall tile

2. Make a list of these things on a piece of paper.

3. Touch each item one at a time. Does each one feel hot or cold? Compare each one to the other objects on your list. Does it feel hotter or colder?

4. Make a list of the objects in order from the hottest to the coldest. Put what you think is the hottest object at the top and the coldest at the bottom.

5. Now place a liquid-crystal thermometer strip on each of the objects.

Liquid crystal ...

A liquid-crystal thermometer is a plastic strip containing a special liquid in clear, thin pockets. The pockets have numbers printed on them. As the temperature rises, the liquid in the pockets changes color and brightens. Then the number on the pocket can be seen. That number is the temperature.

6. Wait a few moments for the temperature to settle. Then read the temperature off the plastic strip.

7. Write down the temperature, in degrees Fahrenheit, for each item on your list.

8. Did you figure out correctly which things were the hottest and which were the coldest?

GLOSSARY

absolute zero The lowest temperature that can ever be reached.

atom A very small piece of a substance.

body temperature The normal temperature of a person, 98.6°F (37°C).

Celsius A temperature scale figured out by Anders Celsius. Also called the centigrade scale.

centigrade A temperature scale based on the temperatures of ice and boiling water. Also called the Celsius scale.

climate The weather a place has over the course of a whole year.

degree A single unit of temperature.

digital thermometer A thermometer that shows the temperature in numbers, like a digital watch.

energy The ability of something to do work (such as pushing or pulling) to make something happen.

Fahrenheit A temperature scale figured out by Daniel Fahrenheit.

filament A thin wire that produces light when heated.

geyser A natural fountain of steam and very hot water.

heat A type of energy that makes something hot or cold.

Kelvin A temperature scale that starts at absolute zero and measures upward in degrees Celsius, or centigrade.

mercury A substance that is used inside many household thermometers.

molecule A group of joined atoms.

Rankine A temperature scale that starts at absolute zero and measures upward in degrees Fahrenheit.

scale A set of equally spaced lines, marked on something like a ruler or thermometer, to help us measure.

steam The gas formed when water is heated to 212°F (100°C).

temperature A measurement of how hot or cold something is. It is not the same as heat.

thermal Describes something of, or caused by, heat.

thermal image A kind of photograph (taken by a thermal camera) that shows areas of heat.

thermometer An instrument for measuring temperature.

thermostat A device that switches heaters and air conditioners on or off to keep a room at the right temperature.

FIND OUT MORE

BOOKS

Carol Ballard, *Heating and Cooling.* Chicago, IL: Heinemann Library, 2008.

Sally Hewitt, *Heat: Too Hot or Too Cold?* Mankato, MN: Stargazer, 2007.

Terry Jennings, *Hot and Cold*. Mankato, MN: Smart Apple, 2009.

Andrew Solway, *Secrets of Heat and Cold.* New York: Marshall Cavendish Benchmark, 2011.

Navin Sullivan, *Temperature.* New York: Marshall Cavendish Benchmark, 2007.

WEBSITES

Physics4Kids: Thermodynamics

A good introduction to temperature scales, heat and heat transfer, and thermal imaging.

http://www.physics4kids.com/files/thermo_scales.html

Temperature conversions–Celsius to Fahrenheit

Convert temperatures from degrees Celsius to degrees Fahrenheit and from Fahrenheit to Celsius.

http://www.sciencemadesimple.com/temperature_conversions.php

Publisher's note to educators and parents: Our editors have carefully reviewed these websites to ensure that they are suitable for students. Many websites change frequently, however, and we cannot guarantee that a site's future contents will continue to meet our high standards of quality and educational value. Be advised that students should be closely supervised whenever they access the Internet.

Answers to questions

Page 9: The temperatures on the thermometer are 106°F, 36°F, and 0°F.

Page 13: 50°F is the same as 10°C. And 30°C is the same as 86°F.

Page 15: If the room temperature is 60°F, the thermostat will switch the heating on; if the room temperature is 70°F, it will switch the heating off.

Page 25: The temperature in April is 50°F; in August, it is 68°F; and in December, the temperature is 30°F.

INDEX